Antiques & Vintage

POEMS BY VAL JONES

Val Jones is a proud resident of St. Michael's Hamlet, Liverpool,
and her poems regularly appear in the Liverpool Echo
newspaper where she is known as Val Jones of L17.

Illustrations by Claire Huntley
www.clairehuntley.com

Contents

1. The Antique Shop
2. Empoli Glass
3. The Serinette
4. Door Knockers
5. Pewter
6. Gold
7. Bakelite
8. Troika
9. Poole Pottery
10. Vintage Posters
11. Imari C17
12. Cocktail Watches
13. The Travelling Penmen
14. Bookmarkers
15. Trench Art
16. Georg Jensen
17. The China Cabinet
18. Shabby Chic
19. Moiré
20. Antiques

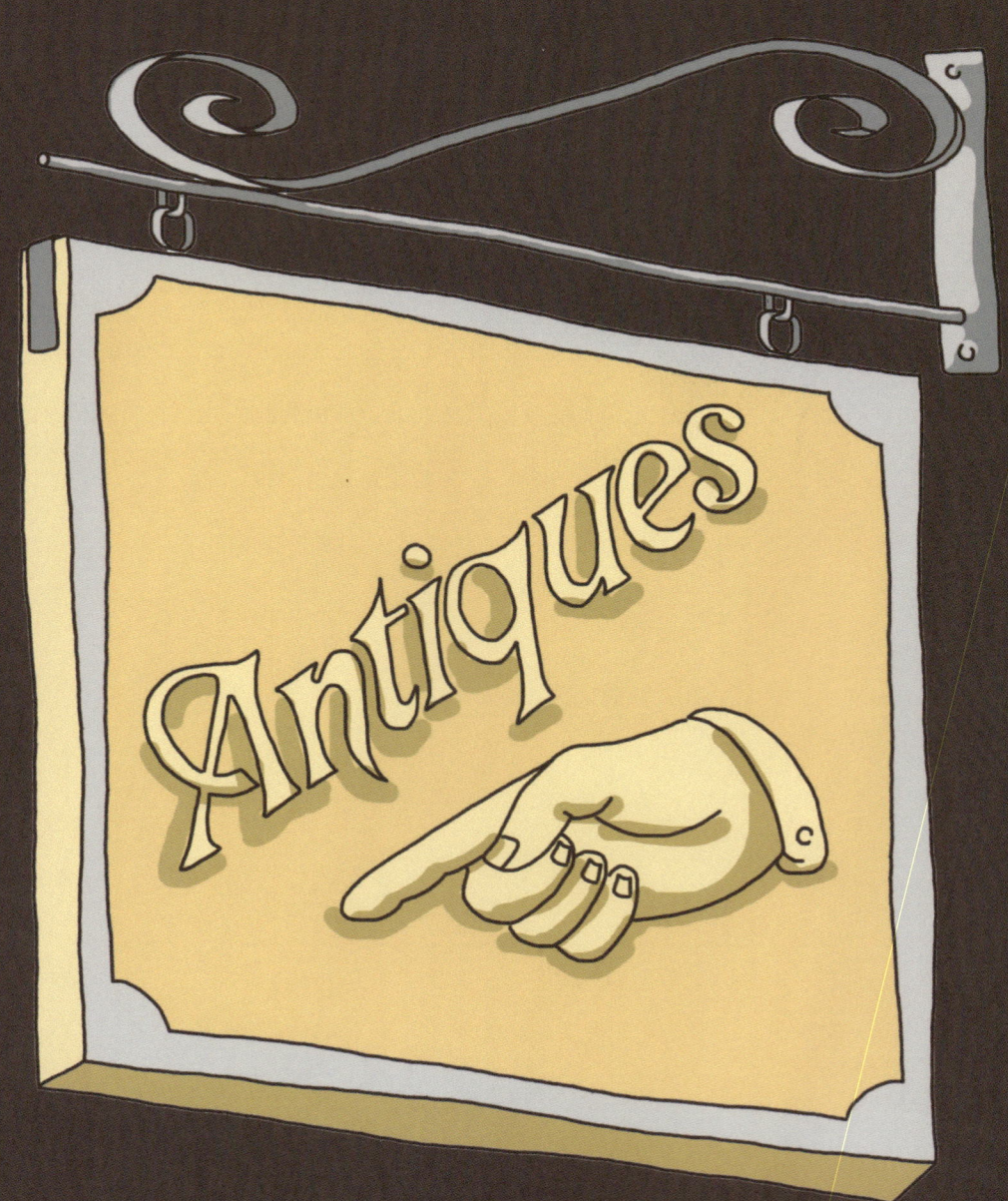

The Antique Shop

What would you say is a genuine antique?
Does it all depend on age?
Yes, it's believed that 100 years or more
Is a true indication and gauge.

First came the cabinet of curiosities
Which the wealthy owned at that time
To display their precious objets d'art
Of a quality that was truly sublime.

Antique shops began when these wealthy people
Were looking to furnish their homes
They stocked furniture, ceramics and rugs
for instance
And artefacts from Greece and Rome.

It all began in London really.
Though there were dealers in main cities too.
It spread to villages and seaside resorts
And they just grew and grew.

Some dealers displayed things in period settings
Others preferred a cluttered display
Antique shops thrived in tourist hotspots
Just as they do today.

The Golden Age for antique shops
Came after the Second World War
In the '60s and '70s antique centres opened
And it developed more and more.

After the '80s demand started to fall
There were reasons for the decline
From the rise of flat-pack furniture
To the repro' furniture line.

Today the antique trade is flourishing
We have shops and centres and fairs.
It's fun, it's exciting, it can be expensive
But if you love something, honestly who cares?

Empoli Glass

Everyone's heard of Murano
But Empoli not so much
It's glassware that's Italian and retro.
But there's little documentation as such.

The most popular are the Genie bottles
Moulded and varying in size.
The lidded bonbon dishes too on their very slim stems
Are another of Empoli's good buys.

Now the colour affects price considerably
Red is very popular today
There's a variation on red known as 'Amberina'
Which is highly desirable I would say.

Now Empoli Verde is green glass
Produced from a mineral nearby
They also made glassware with stripes and swirls
(My favourite - I'm not going to lie).

At least 10 factories sprung up mid-century
Fratelli Betti and Stelvia too
Also Artistica Toscana
Produced glassware that was vibrant and new.

It was a kitsch kind of glassware that was of it's time.
Bold, decorative and colourful too.
It made an impact wherever displayed
And collectors number quite a few.

The Serinette

There was once a Frenchman called
Leonard Boudin
A master craftsman all would agree.
It was about the time of the French Revolution
And he specialised in marquetry.

He designed this amazing little box
Which the French called a Serinette
It's known as a bird organ in English
And is designed to educate your pet.

It was a drawing-room toy for the wealthy
To encourage their caged birds to sing.
A fun and frivolous pastime.
A recreational thing.

Now Boudin was a master craftsman
Who worked in all kinds of wood
Such as walnut, poplar and sycamore
Whatever fine wood he could.

The design was usually of flowers and birds
Often musical instruments too
Its imaginative take on Chinese style
Called 'Chinoiserie' just grew and grew.

Great fun was had in the 18th century
Trying to teach caged birds to sing
Hoping they'd imitate the serinette
Have you ever heard such a thing?

Door Knockers

It was a time before electric bells
When door knockers were on every door
They were also known as 'Rappers'
From a custom that had gone before.

In Tudor times a gentleman
Or the servant by his side
Rapped on a door for entry
With a wooden stave to be allowed inside.

Door knockers are still in use today
But there have been changes too.
By 1850 brass knockers were popular
And of designs there were quite a few.

Medusa with her snaky locks
The Egyptian sphinx as well
The mask of a lion as in Downing St.
A dolphin too I've heard tell.

In Victorian times to muffle a knocker
Took place when the occupant was ill
And straw was even put down in the street
To make things quieter still.

To take off the knocker completely
Was the height of courtesy in those days.
Who would have thought a simple door knocker
Could be significant in such various ways?

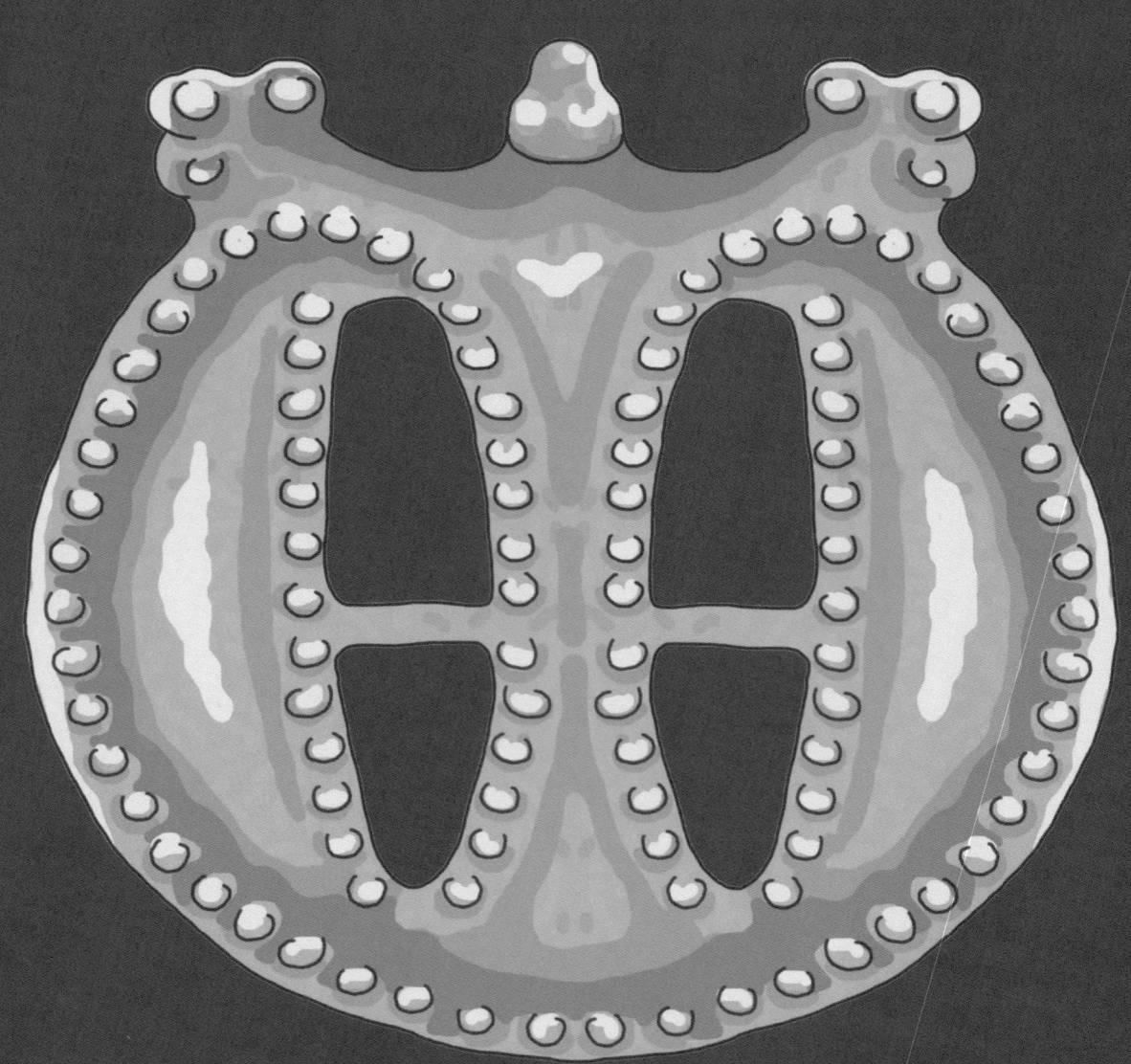

Pewter

It was first made in Britain by the Romans
Dug from Cornish tin mines
For this metal was 95% tin you see
With a beautiful patina and shine.

It fell out of favour but was reintroduced
By Cistercian monks from France
When they came over in the 13th century
And came upon it by chance.

They made pewter chalices for religious use
And made pilgrim badges as well.
These badges are still washed up today
On the banks of the Thames, so people tell.

The largest collection of pewter was found
When a Spanish ship capsized
On the high seas while going to America
To the colonies there, it's surmised.

Now pewter was for everyday use
By all, both rich and poor
It was even used by royalty
For it had this particular allure.

It had this great connection with people
And was even carried around
A pewter spoon in his headband
Was so useful the poor man found.

In the late 19th century collecting pewter
Was popular with gentlemen they say
And even today there's a Pewter Society
For a metal that's here to stay.

Gold

It's decorated the tombs of Pharaohs
To symbolise their might.
It's found in the grandest houses and palaces
Gleaming from morn' 'till night.

Flashes of gold in Mosaics
Glitter in the stream of light
Embellishing the beauty of places of worship
And every holy site.

The effect it creates is powerful
Even a slight brushing of gold leaf
Imagine the gilded opulence of a place
like Versailles
The effect must be beyond belief.

The timeless beauty of a ring of gold
Or a bangle on the wrist
Conveys a feeling of luxury
That is very hard to resist.

It's a golden age in many ways
There's such beauty wherever you go.
But what's really important costs nothing at all
Yet gives us a warm golden glow.

Bakelite

A New York chemist called Leo Baekeland
Discovered the most amazing thing
It was a type of plastic you could mould or change
And make into anything.

It was used for costume jewellery
And from Baekeland derived its name.
Its heyday lay between the '20s and '40s
And achieved a worldwide fame.

It was the top product of early plastic really
And differed in that there was no seam.
It feels rather different if truth be told
And also has a certain sheen.

The most valuable pieces are the
Philadelphia range
Made from panels in different shades.
Necklaces, dress clips and bangles
Were expensive but all the rage.

Now when something becomes really popular
That's when the fakes appear.
However when you find the real thing
It's time to go to the rooftops and cheer.

Troika

They were works of art right from the beginning
Of unique shape and textured design
A modern, architectural, angular look
That the founders considered just fine.

There were 3 founders of Troika pottery
Which started in 1963.
They took over a pottery in St. Ives in Cornwall
In an idyllic spot by the sea.

Benny Sirota, Leslie Illsley and Jan Thompson
Put £1,000 each in the kitty.
Pieces were marked with their initials
Selling in the future at Liberty.

Troika means a set of 3
A nod to the founders maybe.
Some rough textured, others smooth glazed
In appearance contemporary.

The most recognised designs are the Coffin and Wheel
Also the Chimney too.
Troika has always had a strong following
As love of studio ceramics grew.

But by the 80's imported ceramics
Which were plentiful and cheap
Simply flooded the market in Britain
And Troika took a downward leap.

But Troika is still loved by many
And crops up regularly today
In auction houses and antique fairs
And it makes a collector's day.

Poole Pottery

It's known as the home of millionaires
With its golden stretch of sand
But Sandbanks and Poole have a history
Of making ceramics by hand.

Fine clay has been found since Roman times
In this coastal Dorset town
Some Staffordshire potters moved to the area
Hopeful of future renown.

But it was a local builder's merchant
Jesse Carter was his name
Who bought a tile-making factory
Destined to achieve future fame.

It was situated on Poole Harbour
1873 was the date.
It was to be known as Carter and Co.
Who went on to make something great.

1921 was an important year
When Cyril Carter enlisted fresh blood.
Now it was Carter, Stabler and Adams.
Solidarity understood.

Poole Pottery has a distinctive look
And has become a well-known name.
Hand-painted, decorative ware was produced
Achieving world-wide fame.

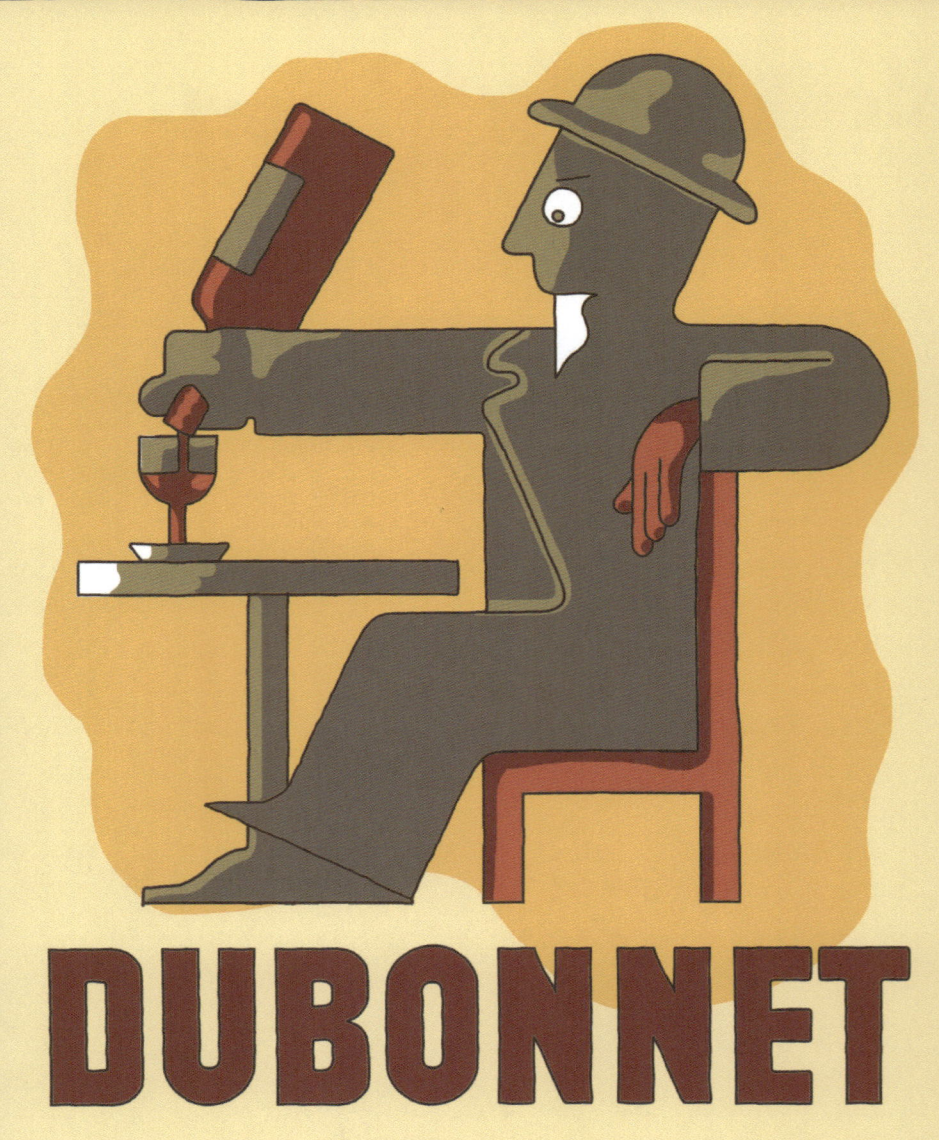

Vintage Posters

Imagine a time before the internet
Before magazines or even TV.
How could firms advertise what they wanted
to sell?
It was almost an impossibility.

Then in stepped the local town crier
To bellow out what was for sale.
Followed by little ads in the press
Often to little avail.

Then something happened in 1870
With the development of the lithographic stone
The printer and artist responsible
Was a Frenchman whose fame's clearly grown.

His name in fact was Jules Chéret
Who did something never done before.
He produced huge colour posters
For which demand grew more and more.

It was a brilliant way of advertising
For industries galore.
The railway, aviation, the car and travel
Are a few but there are plenty more.

They were intended to be pasted on the walls
in town.
A week later another was pasted on top.
Not many survived because the paper was thin.
Fragility was the issue, full stop.

Good quality posters are a rarity
And cost several hundreds of pounds.
Really special ones can be thousands
Because there aren't many around.

In this Digital Age we're bombarded by adverts
Encouraging us to spend every day.
But a great poster can be the most exciting
purchase
A true work of art on display.

Imari C17

Imari was a traditional style
Of Japanese porcelain then.
Even today it's produced in Derby
But how did it start and when?

Near the port of Imari in the Arita area
Of Japan 400 years ago
Kaolin a type of clay was found.
From then it was all systems go.

Japan traded through the Dutch East
India Company.
Soon Dutch traders introduced designs
of their own.
A Dutch vase of flowers for instance.
The seeds of European Imari were sown.

The style was developed in underglaze blue
With an overglaze of rust red and gilt.
Producers in Delft started to make it
And a whole new industry was built.

Europeans demanded similar designs
So German and French porcelain emerged.
Chelsea and Worcester were the leading makers
Spode too as British interest surged.

They introduced familiar images
Like the English rose and garden bird
Replacing the dragons and hibiscus trees
Of which British potters hadn't seen or heard.

So Imari became a true British style
Adapted from a Japanese design
In demand all over the world
A truly indicative sign.

Cocktail Watches

They were the most exquisite time pieces.
Designed to be seen and admired
With the added benefit of telling the time.
It was jewellery of which you never tired.

They were dressier and more glamorous than
normal watches
Designed to accompany evening wear
They had a very small dial encircled with jewels
Which were often expensive and rare.

There was nothing discreet about
cocktail watches
A sign of status for the wealthy few.
Produced by top jewellers like Cartier and Tiffany
Van Cleef and Arpels too.

They were all the rage in the '20s and '30s
But the dress code is less formal today.
Also maintenance of such a tiny mechanism
Would need a specialist watchmaker I'd say.

So for a moment in time the little cocktail watch
In fashionable circles took centre stage
It was beautiful, it was practical and rather
a novelty.
No wonder it was all the rage.

The Travelling Penmen

Calligraphy in Victorian times
Was the accomplishment of only a few
So Penmen travelled to remote villages
To help the illiterate too.

They inscribed their names in their family Bibles
In Prayer Books and Hymn Books too
And wrote household texts to hang in
their cottages
Their reputation just grew and grew.

Funeral Cards obtained at the undertakers
Were valued by both rich and poor.
They were bordered in black with heartfelt verses
And had a certain melancholy allure.

But the principal source of income
For the travelling Penmen came
From decorating farmers' wagons
And inscribing on them their name.

In Thomas Hardy's 'Far From The
Madding Crowd'
Gabriel Oak was the Penman in that.
It was said he could write with beautiful flourishes
And long tails like that of a cat.

By the end of the century these Penmen
had vanished
Itinerant artists too.
Education now was much more widespread
And not only for the few.

National and Church Schools were established
And we enter a different age.
The travelling Penmen had played their past.
It was time to turn the page.

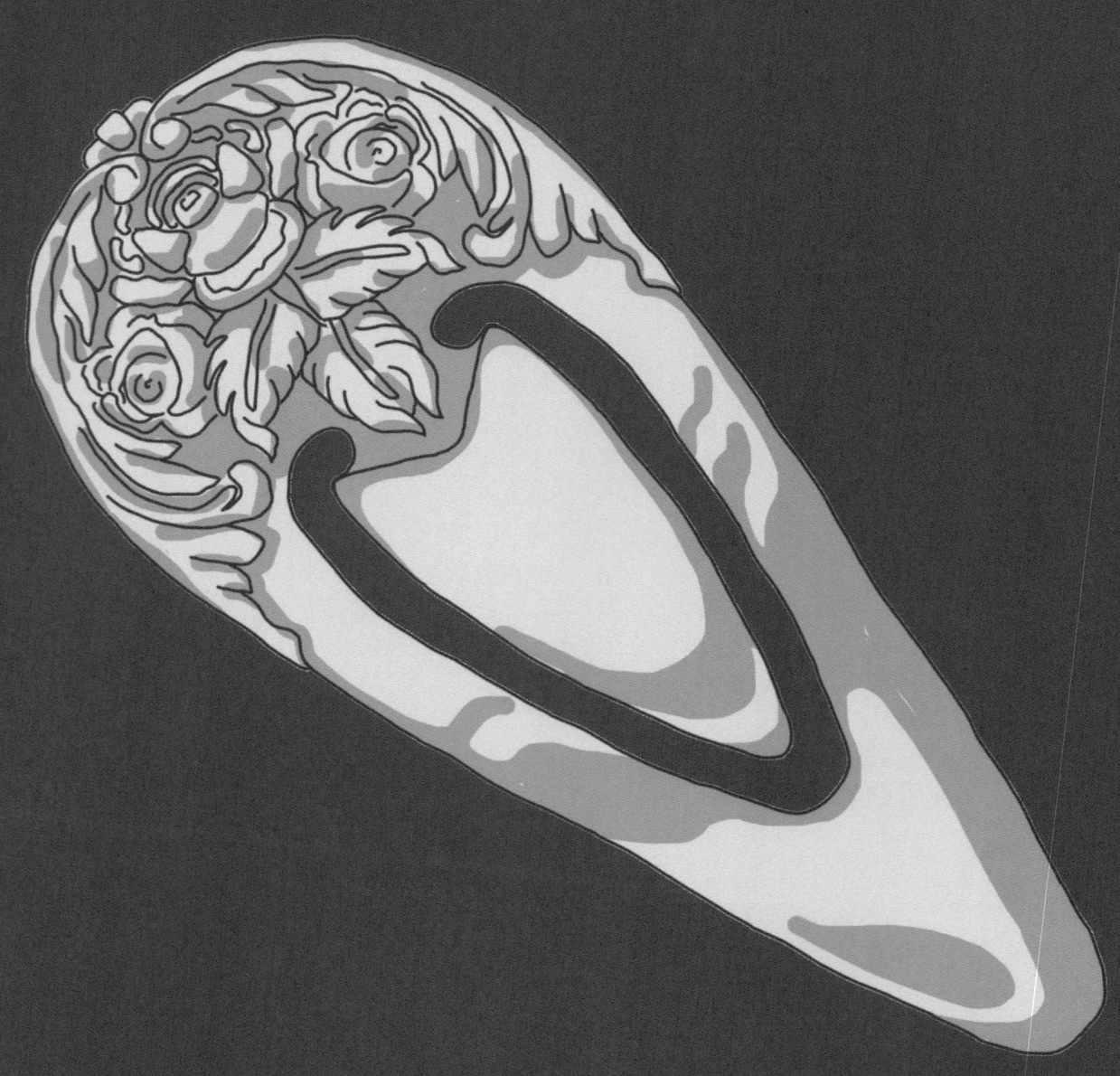

Bookmarkers

The companion of Bibles for centuries
And devotional prayer books as well.
There was a widespread use in Victorian times
By both rich and poor it's heard tell.

We talk of the popularity of bookmarkers
In their Bibles for going to church.
Silk for the rich in blue or purple
Cardboard for the poor.

As well as religious bookmarkers
There were sentimental ones too.
Made as gifts or love tokens
A parlour past time for the wealthy few.

The commercial bookmarker was hugely popular
It was often given for free.
A form of advertising that also gave pleasure
To the entire community.

It was often found in a box of Pears soap
Or a Huntley and Palmers tin
Also with Cherry Blossom polish
It was an advertising win-win.

Bars of music were often on markers
Quotations from Shakespeare too.
Favourite lines from hymns or songs
Their popularity just grew and grew.

Trench Art

Creating decorative items from the debris of war
Has been known since the beginning of time.
For scrap metal was strewn over hundreds
of miles.
To use it was certainly no crime.

Collectors call it 'Trench Art'
Which flourished in the First World War
The name however is misleading
And it was afterwards that interest soared.

Trench Art is really an umbrella term
Covering embroidery and jewellery too
Cigarette cases, ash trays and model tanks
Of religious items there were quite a few.

Artillery shells are the most frequently seen
(As in the Imperial War Museum today)
Models of military vehicles and equipment
Permanently on display.

They were often made by prisoners of war
And soldiers recovering from the fray.
Each piece tells a story
That resonates today.

They highlight the human side of war
How it's personal to everyone.
We'll never know each story
Of how the war was won.

Shabby Chic

It's almost a particular decorating style
Though it's not always somebody's choice.
Some say it evolved in the post-war period
When affordability had the main voice.

Incomes were reduced and the philosophy then
Was one of 'make do and mend'
One shrugged one's shoulders at scratches
on furniture
It's not as if the world's at an end.

Some call it 'picturesque decrepitude'
Beautiful things that were far past their best.
Spartan bathrooms - just soap and a towel
Though the towel did bear the fancy crest.

Turkish carpets worn and faded
Loose covers laundered time and again
There's a sense of timelessness in homes like this
As if left since who knows when?

Contemporary lives in Shabby Chic houses
Where things are pleasingly worn.
Inside you'll find real beauty
A new way of living is born.

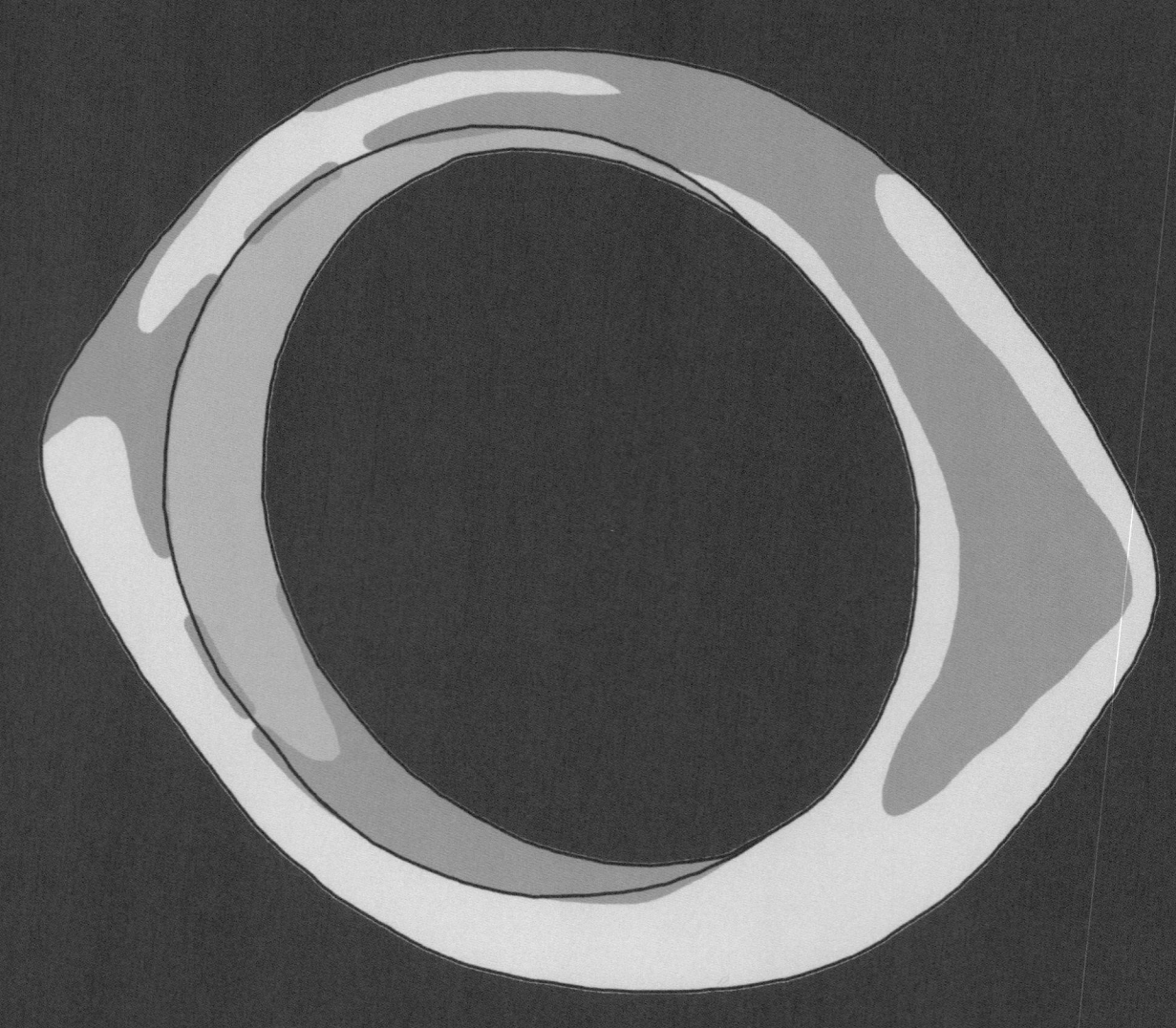

Georg Jensen

He was influenced by Scandinavian design philosophy
That of making high quality things
Unfussy and affordable
Such as brooches, necklaces and rings.

We're talking of a 20th century designer
Georg Jensen from Denmark was his name.
Influenced by our Arts and Crafts movement
He went on to achieve worldwide fame.

He worked mainly in silver
And made jewellery still popular today.
Influenced by nature, pared back and organic
His vision is here to stay.

He died in the 1930s
But the firm continued his vision.
If you want to buy something elegant yet simple
You will not regret the decision.

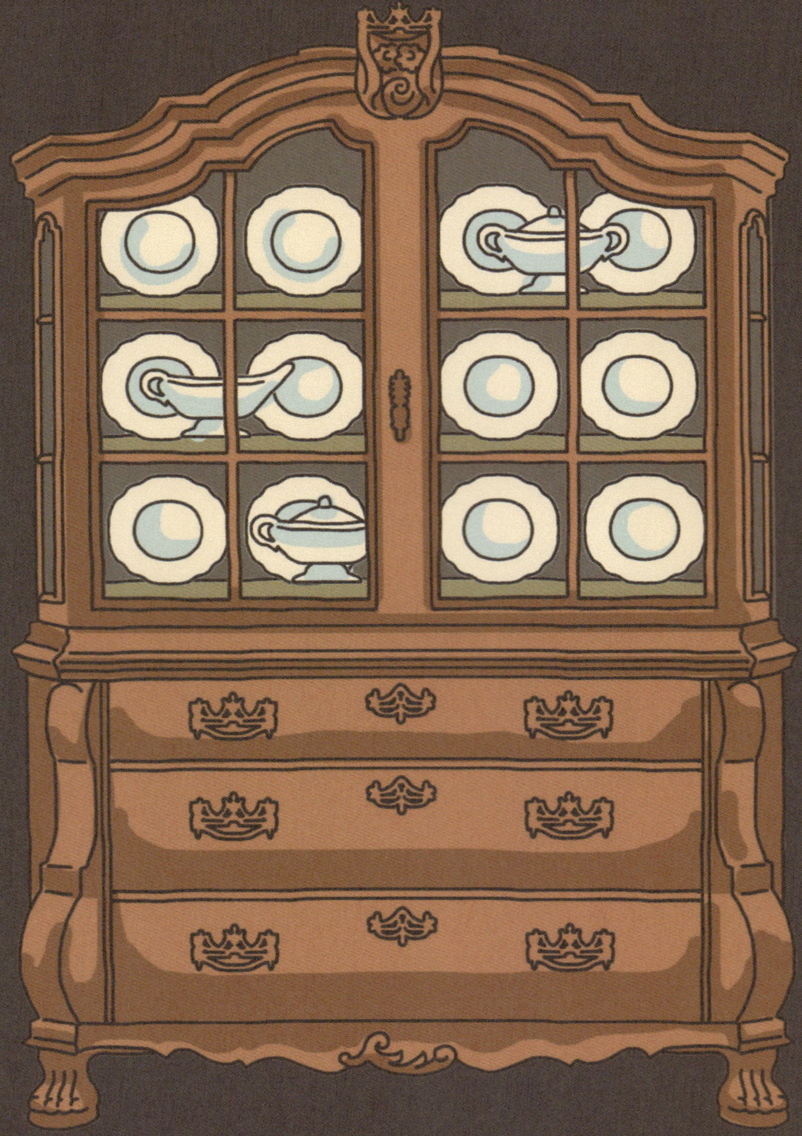

The China Cabinet

They brought a blast of Caribbean colour
To a grey post-war Britain at the time
From a harsh and demanding life in the cane fields
Where they had little free time.

Saturday nights had been precious
A time for music and dance.
Colourful dress, good food and drink
Part time whenever they had chance.

Life was hard too in post-war Britain
Opportunities for work were rare.
Where could they dance and socialise together?
Very few places to be fair.

So the home was very important
For entertainment when they had leisure
A place for getting together
Special times that they were to treasure.

There was one essential item of furniture
Still to be found today.
The one item of precious furniture
Where fine china was on display.

And that is the china cabinet
Where the best tea set was kept safe and sound
To be brought out on special occasions
And to be proudly passed around.

It wasn't just something to drink from
It was the symbol of a better life
To be offered proudly to visitors
Behind them the times of struggle and strife.

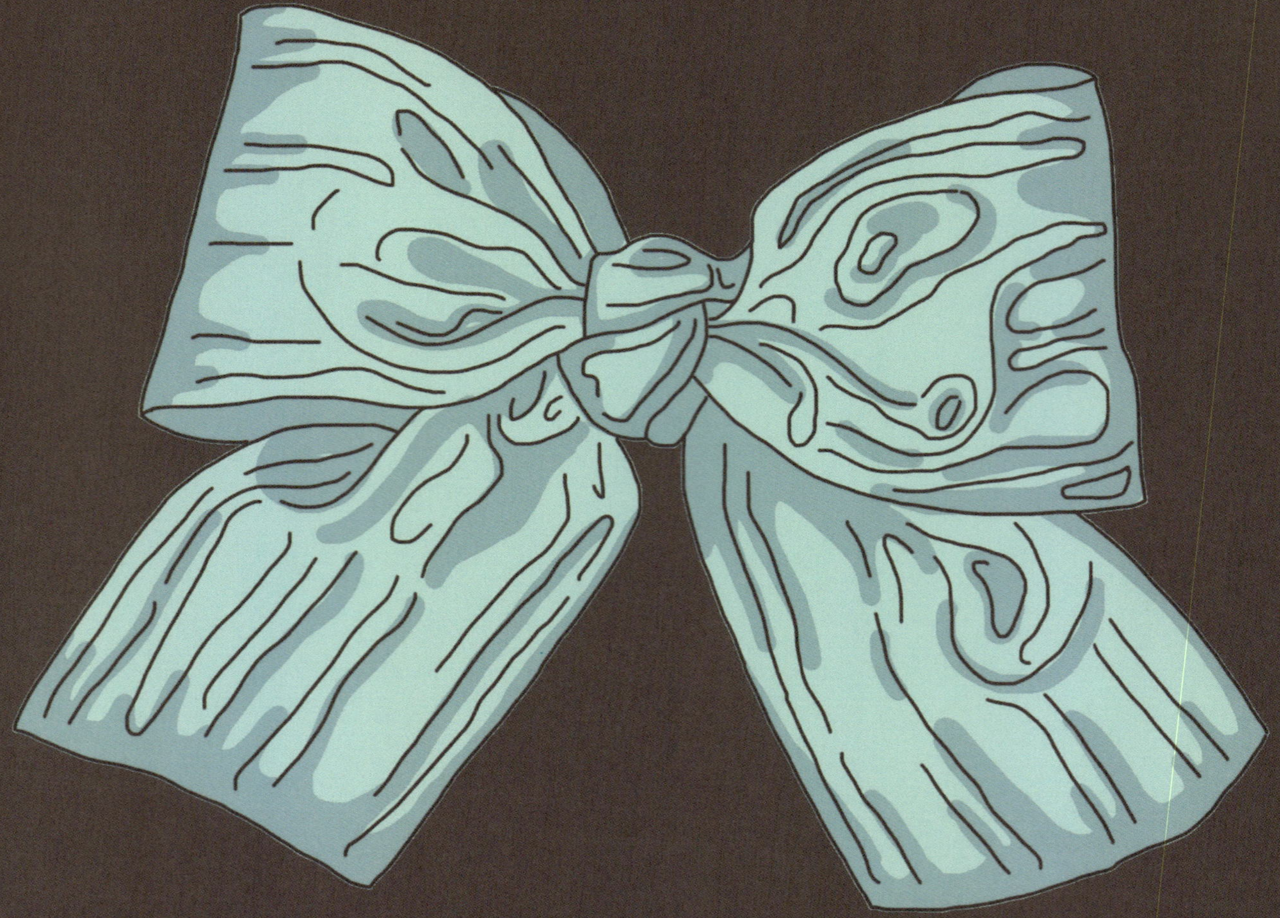

Moiré

It's such an interesting textile
First made in China they say
For the country abounded in the most skilful
of weavers
Who produced fine cloth every day.

Now Moiré has a rippling look
And is made in the most fascinating way.
Heat is applied with rollers
Onto the folded cloth they say.

From the 17th to the 19th century
It was a sign of formal dress
Queen Victoria herself wore a blue Moiré sash
And Peter the Great no less.

Used by Dior and Laurent in haute couture
It is used in interiors too
In Hampton Court Palace in the 1600s
To the White House to mention a few.

The V and A possesses a fantastic dress
Made entirely from Moiré it's said.
It's surely a silk for the ages
That will never lose its street cred'.

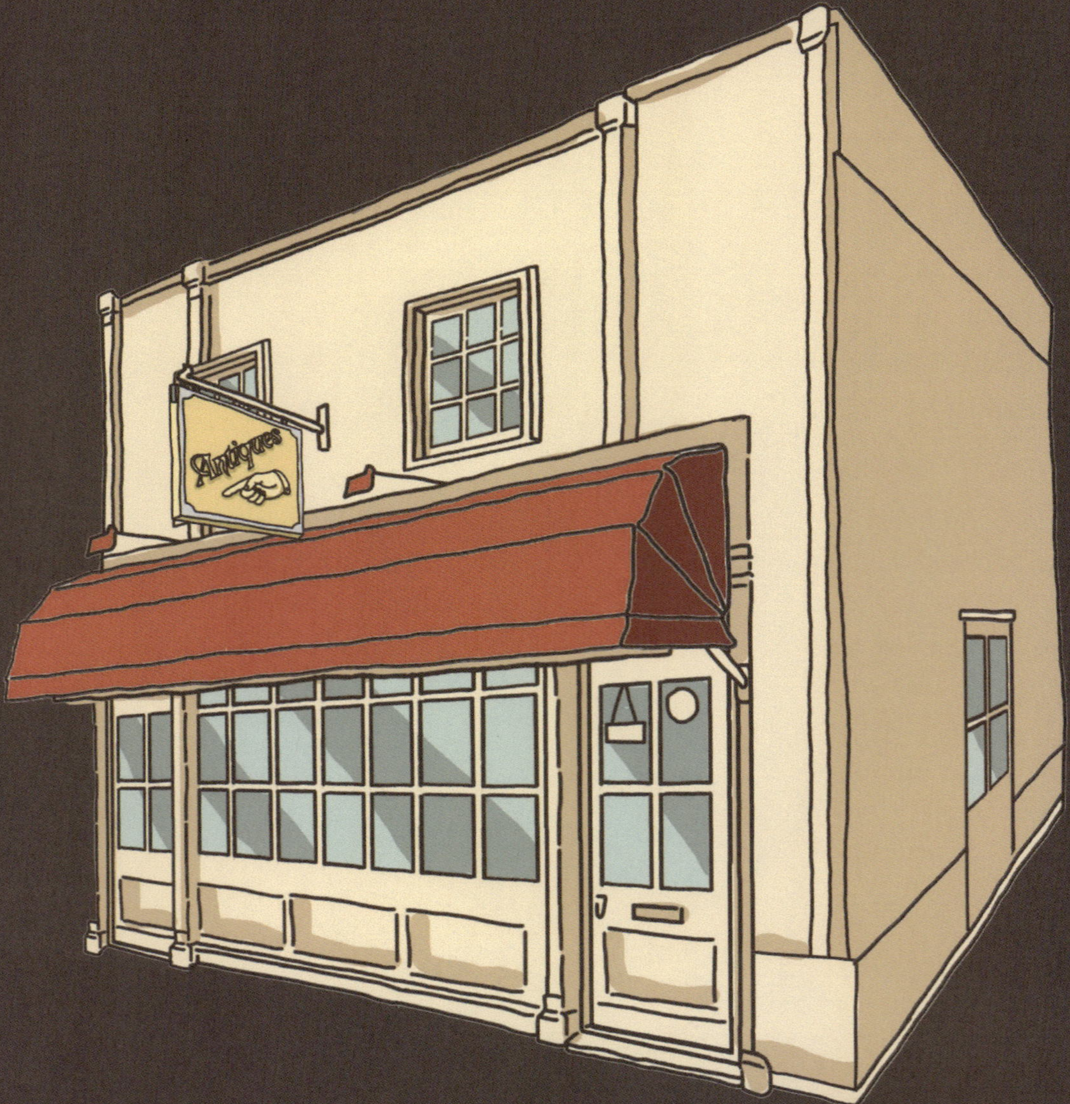
Antiques

Antiques

Antiques is a word derived from Latin
As so many English words are.
'Antiquus' means aged, honest and venerable
'Of the old stamp' more desirable by far.

Many of us regard them as works of art
Bearing the history of a far-off time
To be lovingly cherished and admired each day
To do otherwise would be a crime.

Now some people like things shiny and new
Each to their own, we say.
Ancient, or modern, whatever the provenance
Antiques are here to stay.

Poems written by Val Jones of L17

Illustrations by Claire Huntley
www.clairehuntley.com

Further books in this series

Available on Amazon, featuring paintings by Dominic Burkhalter (dominicburkhalter.com) and illustrations by Claire Huntley (clairehuntley.com)

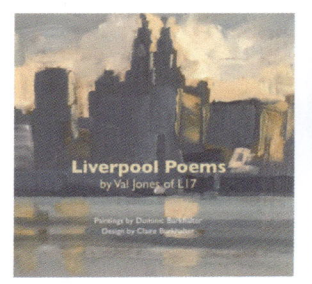

Liverpool Poems

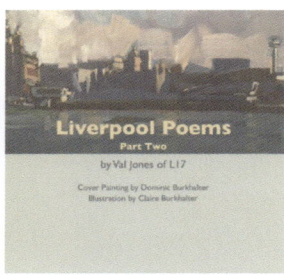

Liverpool Poems: Part Two

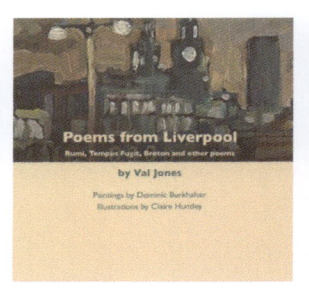

Poems from Liverpool:
Rumi, Tempus Fugit, Breton and other poems

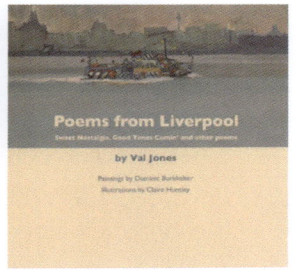

Poems from Liverpool:
Sweet Nostalgia, Good Times Comin' and other poems

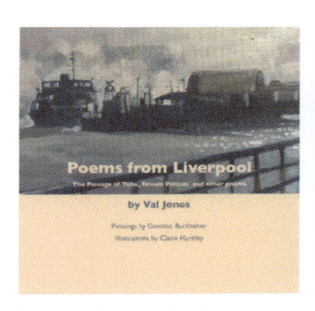

Liverpool Poems: The Passage of Time, Dream Palaces and other poems

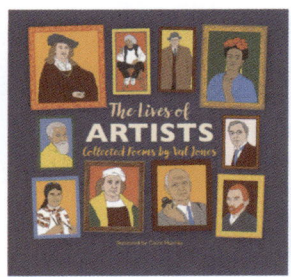

The Lives of Artists:
Collected Poems

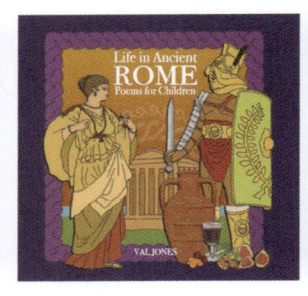

Life in Ancient Rome:
Poems for Children

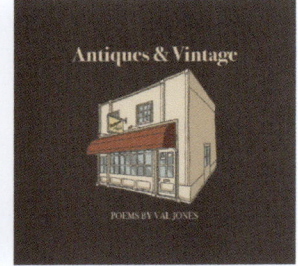

Antiques & Vintage: Poems

Printed in Great Britain
by Amazon